DATE DUE

CONTINENTS

Australia

Mary Virginia Fox

Heinemann Library
Chicago, Illinois

Designed by Joanna Hinton-Malivoire and Q2A Creative
Printed in China by South China Printing Company

10 09 08 07 06
10 9 8 7 6 5 4 3 2 1

New edition ISBN: 1-4034-8542-9 (hardcover)
 1-4034-8550-X (paperback)

The Library of Congress has cataloged the first edition as follows:
Fox, Mary Virginia.
 Australia / Mary Virginia Fox.
 p. cm. – (Continents)
 Includes bibliographical references (p.) and index.
 ISBN 1-57572-449-9
 1. Australia – Juvenile literature. [1. Australia.] I. Title. II. Continents
(Chicago, Ill.)
DU96 .F7 2001
994–dc21

00-011467

Acknowledgments
The publishers are grateful to the following for permission to reproduce copyright material: Animals Animals: Hans & Judy Beste p. 15; Bruce Coleman Inc.: Norman Owen Tomalin, pp. 14, 23, Hans Reinhard p. 16, Eric Crichton p. 21, Bob Burch p. 27; Corbis: Theo Allofs p.11, Patrick Ward p. 25; Earth Scenes: Dani/Jeske pp. 5, 17, Michael Fogden, p. 6; Getty Images: Photographer's Choice/ Ross Woodhall p. 8; Peter Arnold: J.P. Perrero p. 12, John Cancalosi p. 19; Photo Researchers: Georg Gerster p. 22; A. Flowers & L. Newman, p. 29; Tony Stone: Robin Smith p. 24, Doug Armand p. 28.

Cover photograph of Australia, reproduced with permission of Science Photo Library/ Worldsat International and J. Knighton.

The publishers would like to thank Kathy Peltan, Keith Lye, and Nancy Harris for their assistance in the preparation of this book.

Every effort has been made to contact copyright holders of any material reproduced in this book. Any omissions will be rectified in subsequent printings if notice is given to the publishers.

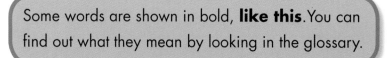

Some words are shown in bold, **like this**. You can find out what they mean by looking in the glossary.

Contents

Where Is Australia?

A continent is a very large area of land. There are seven continents in the world. Australia is the smallest continent. Australia is below the **Equator**. The Equator is an imaginary line around the center of Earth.

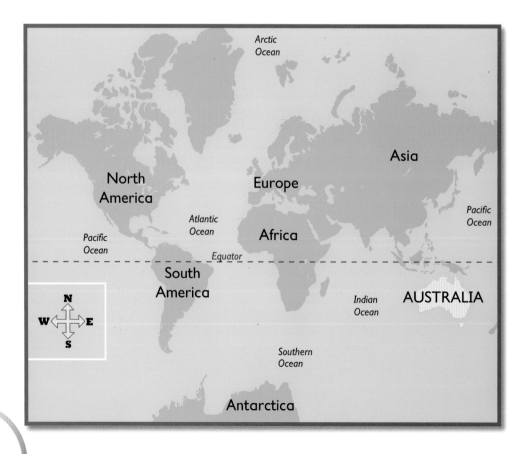

▲ *Australia is a huge island surrounded by sea.*

Australia is a large island, so it is surrounded by large bodies of water. The Indian Ocean is to the west. The Southern Ocean is to the south. The Pacific Ocean is to the east. To the south is the small island state of Tasmania. This is also part of Australia.

Weather

In Australia, winter lasts from June to September. This is summertime in the United States. The weather in most of Australia is very hot and dry. In summer it is not unusual for the temperature to reach over 100 °F (38 °C). There is a short rainy season.

The dry, bare country away from the Australian coast is called the **outback**.

▲ *The land of the Australian outback is very dry.*

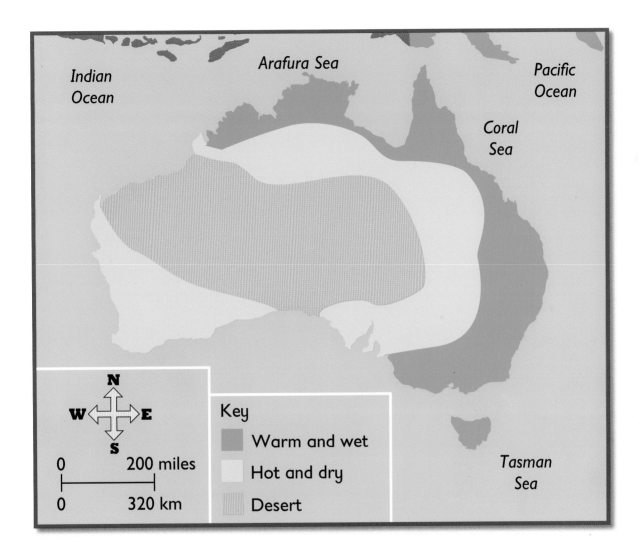

Northern Australia is close to the **Equator**.
Near the Equator, the weather is hot and wet.
In the southern part of the continent, winters
can be very cold. It sometimes snows in
southeastern Australia.

Mountains

▲ *People ski in New Zealand.*

Australia has only a few high mountains.
Its highest mountain is Mount Kosciuszko.
Southeast of Australia is the country of New
Zealand. New Zealand has many steep,
snow-covered **peaks**. Australians sometimes
go skiing and snowboarding there.

Australia has mountains called the Great Dividing Range. On one side of the mountains it is hot and dry. On the other side, it is warm and wet. Most Australians live in cities on the coasts. Few people live in the **deserts** of central Australia.

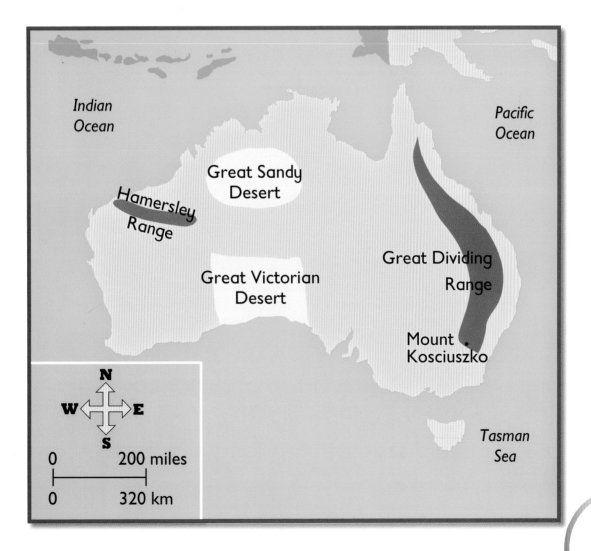

Indian Ocean

Pacific Ocean

Great Sandy Desert

Hamersley Range

Great Dividing Range

Great Victorian Desert

Mount Kosciuszko

N
W — E
S

0 — 200 miles

0 — 320 km

Tasman Sea

Rivers

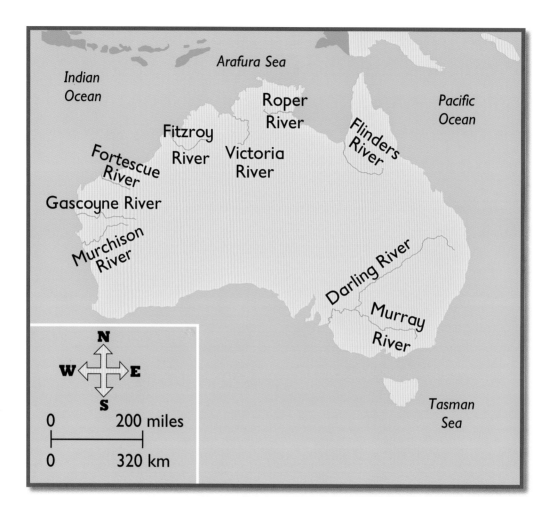

Australia's main rivers are around the edge of the country. The Murray and Darling rivers join to make the Murray-Darling River. Some of Australia's best farming land is in the Murray Valley.

About two-thirds of Australia is made up of **desert**. The **climate** there is very dry. Many of central Australia's rivers dry up completely during the hot summer months.

▲ *This river has dried up completely.*

Lakes

Lake Eyre is the largest lake in Australia. This **saltwater** lake is almost empty for most of the year. Many Australian lakes dry up for part of the year. This is because there is very little rain.

Lake Eyre has only filled up completely three times in the last 100 years.

▲ *Lake Eyre is in South Australia.*

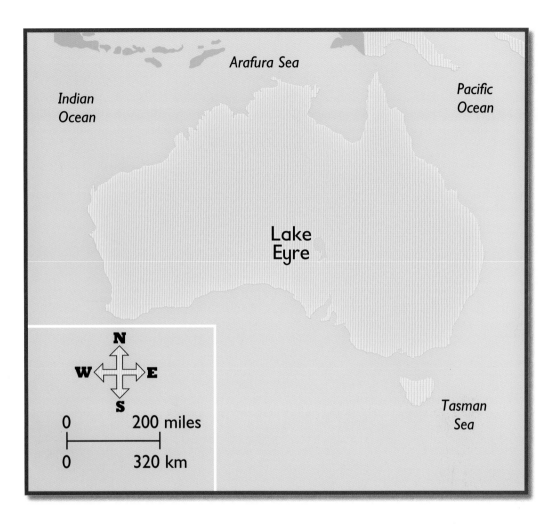

Lake Eyre is the lowest part of Australia. Many tourists visit it. Some of them camp in a large park that surrounds the lake. When the lake is dry, the bottom of it is covered with salt and clay.

Animals

The emu can run 30 miles (48 kilometers) per hour.

▲ *This emu is galloping in a field.*

Some very unusual animals live in Australia. The emu is a bird that can weigh more than 100 pounds (45 kilograms). It can be as tall as a person. It cannot fly.

Kangaroos and koalas are only found in Australia. The mothers have **pouches** for carrying their babies. A baby kangaroo is called a joey. The duck-billed platypus has **webbed** feet and a flat beak, like a duck.

▼ *This shows a kangaroo and a joey.*

Baby kangaroos are tiny when they are born. They crawl up into their mother's pouch. They stay there for about six months.

15

Plants

Eucalyptus, or gum trees, grow in many parts of Australia. These trees can grow in all the different **climates** of Australia. **Rainforests** are found in the north and northeast of the continent.

There are more than 500 types of gum trees.

▲ *Gum trees grow in Australia.*

▲ *Kangaroo paw is prickly.*

Wild flowers, such as the kangaroo paw, grow in western Australia. They grow during the rainy season. The seeds of one type of **desert** plant lie in the hot desert for many years, waiting for rain.

People

Around 40,000 years ago, people from Southeast Asia began to arrive in northern Australia. The first people to live in Australia were called **Aboriginal people**. They lived in Australia for thousands of years.

▼ *These are aboriginal children.*

There were once about 250 Australian languages. Only a few are used today.

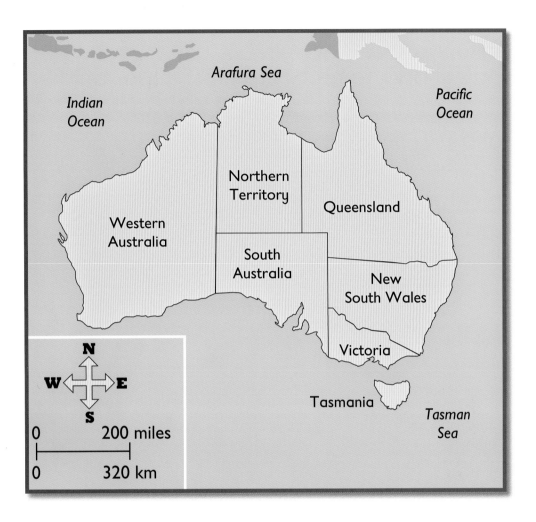

The British explorer Captain Cook sailed to Australia over 200 years ago. Then, many people from Europe came to live there. They divided the main land into six areas. Many people who lived there began to speak English.

Cities

This map shows some of the most important cities in Australia. The **capital city** of Australia is Canberra. Darwin is a busy port and a center for **mining**. The Gold Coast has beautiful beaches and many large hotels.

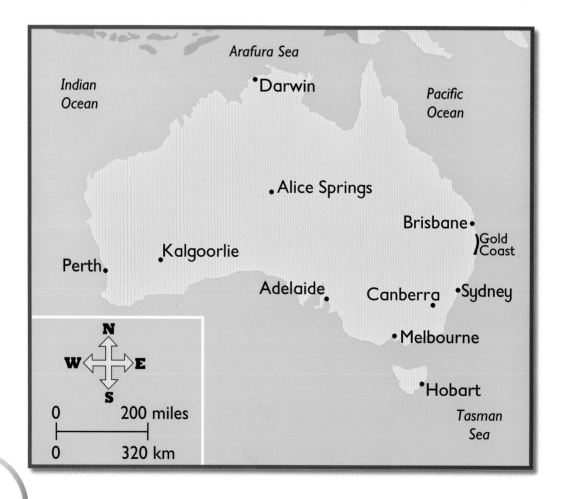

These streetcars take people around the city center.

▲ *Streetcars ride in Melbourne.*

Melbourne is the second largest city in Australia (after Sydney). It was built with money from gold mining. Now, Melbourne is an important center for art, theater, and music. There are three colleges, as well as many offices and factories.

Large yachts take part in sailing races in the sea around Perth.

▲ *Perth is in Western Australia.*

Perth is the largest city on Australia's west coast. The city and its **suburbs** are known for their beautiful beaches and parks. Perth is also a popular place to go **yachting**.

Most Australians live in the cities along the coasts. Some people live close to the city center. But many people's homes are in the suburbs surrounding the cities.

There is plenty of space in Australia, so the houses usually have large yards.

▲ *This Australian home is in the suburbs.*

In the Country

Away from the cities, the bare land of the Australian **outback** stretches for thousands of miles. Cattle and sheep farmers live on huge **ranches** called stations.

Towns in Australia are usually very far apart.

▲ *Children use a radio to take classes.*

Most children in the outback live far away from the nearest school. Their classes are on a radio or a computer, not in a school. If people become sick in the outback, a "flying doctor" travels in a small plane to see them.

Famous Places

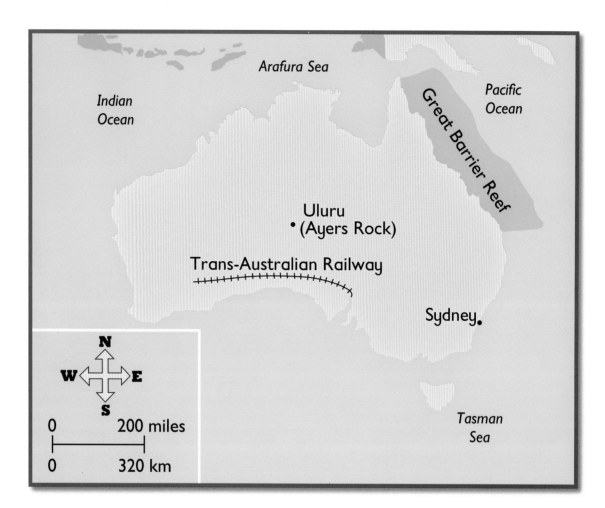

The Trans-Australian Railway runs through the **outback**. Before it was built, people had to walk across the **desert** or ride on camels. Today, many people also choose to travel by airplane to get from one city to another.

The Sydney Opera House sits on the shores of Sydney Harbor. Sydney is the oldest and largest city in Australia. The Olympic Games were held there in the year 2000.

The roof of the Sydney Opera House looks like the sails of **yachts**.

▲ *This is the Sydney Opera House.*

27

Uluru is a mountain of red rock in central Australia. It is also called Ayers Rock. Uluru is a sacred place for the **Aboriginal people**. It has many rock paintings on its surface. At sunset, it looks purple.

Uluru is the Aboriginal name for this rock. It means "many heads."

▲ *Ayers Rock is also called Uluru.*

The Great Barrier Reef is the world's largest coral reef.

▲ *The Great Barrier Reef.*

The Great Barrier **Reef** runs along the northeast coast of Australia. Coral is made from the skeletons of millions of tiny sea creatures. It grows in many shapes and colors. Thousands of different types of fish swim among the coral.

Fast Facts

Australia's highest mountains

Name of mountain	Height in feet	Height in meters	Australian state
Mount Kosciuszko	7,310	2,228	New South Wales
Mount Townsend	7,247	2,209	New South Wales
Mount Twynam	7,201	2,195	New South Wales
Rams Head	7,185	2,190	New South Wales
Etheridge Ridge	7,152	2,180	New South Wales

Australia's longest rivers

Name of river	Length in miles	Length in kilometers	Australian state
Murray River	1,570	2,520	New South Wales, South Australia
Murrumbidgee River	980	1,575	New South Wales
Darling River	860	1,390	New South Wales
Lachlan River	850	1,370	New South Wales

Australia's record breakers

Towns in Australia can be 93 miles (150 kilometers) apart.

The Great Barrier Reef is the world's largest coral **reef**. It stretches for 1,243 miles (2,000 kilometers).

Australia produces a quarter of the world's wool. There are about eight times as many sheep as people in Australia!

Glossary

Aboriginal people first people to live in Australia

capital city city where government leaders work

climate type of weather a place has

desert hot, dry area with very little rain

Equator imaginary circle around the exact middle of Earth

mining digging up things from under Earth's surface

outback land in Australia away from the cities

peak highest part of a mountain

pouch part on the front of a kangaroo where a baby is kept

rainforest thick forest that has heavy rain all year round

ranch very large farm where animals are kept

reef line of underwater rocks or coral close to the surface of the sea

saltwater water that is salty, like the sea

suburb area of houses at the edge of a big city

webbed feet where the toes are joined together, like a duck's feet

yacht sailing boat

More Books to Read

Parker, Vic. *We're from Australia*. Chicago: Heinemann Library, 2006.

Royston, Angela. *Deserts*. Chicago: Heinemann Library, 2005.

Spilsbury, Louise and Richard. *Watching Kangaroos in Australia*. Chicago: Heinemann Library, 2006.

Index